JOURNAL OF THE LAKE

Excerpts from a Seventieth Year

ALICE RYERSON HAYES

Open Books
Berkeley, California

Credits:

"The Monet Show," *Prairie Schooner,* Spring 1993
"Unnaming as a Preparation for Winter," *Prairie
    Schooner,* Summer 1994
"Seeing Birds," *Women's Review of Books,* Summer 1994
"Imagining Water," *Women's Review of Books,* Summer
    1994
"My Childhood Is My Firstborn Child," *Spoon River
    Poetry Review,* Winter 1994
"Armchair Veldt," *Whetstone,* Winter 1993
"On the Dock," *Primavera,* Spring 1995
"6 A.M.," *Passager,* Winter 1996

Also by Alice Ryerson
    Excavation, Kelsey Street Press, 1980
    Matrimonial Picnic, 1984
    New and Selected Poems, Spoon River Poetry Press, 1987
Forthcoming in 1997, under the name Alice Ryerson
Hayes, and illustrated by Jeffrey Apt:
    Water, Bookwrights Press

Open Books
1631 Grant Street
Berkeley, CA 94703

CONTENTS

PREFACE

When I was seventy a huge window opened out of my life. There is nothing metaphorical about this window. It's twelve feet wide and opens onto a view such as I've never lived with before. When I look out I see layers of landscape receding into the distance, with Lake Michigan taking up most of the space between the park in the foreground, and the far horizon, all made endlessly various by weather and birds. The water is transfigured by wind and light and temperature.

Ore boats pass on the horizon. I see the smoke of the steel mills rising heavily into the sky. Park buildings with towers look like crusader castles, and storms turn the shore into a romantic rocky coast. I watch curious dramas enacted in the park: a dog howls alone on the beach, a figure stands motionless at the end of the promontory for a whole afternoon, there are sudden cries and lights in the night. Sometimes, out of the time when I was a child in Chicago, where the presence of the lake is always felt and everyone knows which way is east, pieces of my past and members of my family appear, connected to the lake by watery trains of thought.

My husband and I moved here in the early fall. This book is about the first six months I spent watching the changing lake in winter. The window I look out of is in a retirement building in Chicago, so it's about human winter too. The book is the consequence of weather and winter kindling fresh wonders and new poems in my seventy-year-old mind.

NOVEMBER

I TURN INTO A LAKE

The lake breaks me open
with its gulls and ducks,
its pinks going gray and grays going pink.
Never the same.
Reaching towards the horizon
I become a sheet of water, flown over,
assembled into waves,
a lapper of sand and a smasher of rocks.
I'm a blue current rounding a point.
I shimmer in patches, and easily
hold up two big ships.
My boundaries become foggy.
I'm not sure whether more of me is water
than was planned in the beginning.

I'm about to disintegrate
into billions of molecules
of H_2O, when suddenly
the sight of a black crow settling in a bare tree
scoops me out of the fog and condenses me
into a woman sitting in bed
with a pencil and paper in her lap.

There's rain against the window; waves are bashing the rocks. Squalls make dark patches on the water. As the sky darkens, the breaking waves become iridescent and the air fills with melodrama.

The curtain has just gone up!

PHOTOGRAPHIC SELF-PORTRAIT
To a Photographer on his 80th Birthday

Being born is like a lens opening.
The time-exposure starts
and there you are, pop!
beginning to develop.
The light starts doing its job.
Everything changes while you record,
a slow story telling itself
in a dark room.
All the texture gets put in,
the dark and light alternations,
the ups and downs,
worn places and highlights.
Finally I can see
a rough flight of steps going somewhere
and getting there. They climb
right up the life of that person
who was born in the beginning
when the camera said snick snack
and you were named Jack.

There's an icy fringe along that line between beach and water where the gulls like to stand. Even so, every morning a few birds come from their homes in the steaming dumps to check out the lake. They fly along the shore for a short distance looking for news and then flap disconsolately home.

ORE BOATS AT THE END OF THE SEASON

The ore boats are hurrying north along the horizon
like can-openers at the lake's rim.
Now at the end of November
the lake is thickening towards stillness.
Black birds spray out of the trees and are gone.
A squirrel is trying for the last pod of seeds
but the ore boats aren't loitering in their harbors.

Even the smallest are going north
to Iron Mountain and the Soo
to load ore for the winter mills.
Their radios have heard the weather reports:
cold is coming down the lake.
Cold is making the water slow
and the waves weak as old hands.

The ore boats are moving as fast as they can,
one after another in procession
through this crescendo of cold.
They are racing the ice one more time
before their captains stop trying.
It's hard for men to breathe this air
even with scarves tied over their mouths.

The lake is all a-shine at the edges. There are little unstressed waves in a view I never have to worry about or take care of. The ducks and seagulls are floating together in integrated groups. The ducks dive and disappear, while the seagulls bob on small waves nearby. Perhaps they're waiting for a reappearing duck to drop a minnow, although I've never seen a seagull eat on the water. Maybe they just like the ducks' company.

RUMINATION

Since we moved across town
to this apartment all of the thumps
are different. The rhythmic exercises
of upstairs George are replaced
by the soft door closings
of Ruth and Merlin next door.

I understand the feelings
of cows in their stalls.
I am consoled like them by lives
unfolding in compartments beside mine,
comforted by the soft lowing
of neighbors munching their hay.

There is nothing out there except the tops of two trees shrinking towards me. Beyond them is as much emptiness as I've ever let my eyes out into.

An enormous crow beats like terror past my window. I see the fluting of feathers at the tips of his dark black wings.

People with foresight who have studied the matter needn't go through the tedious business of dying. They can just *be dead*.

But the two treetops anchor me to the earth. With a scribble of twigs they void the void which the fog makes.

UNNAMING AS A PREPARATION FOR WINTER
for Susan Moon

See the old woman sitting on a park bench?
The park lies around her, dismantling itself for winter.
They are both preparing to be minimalists.
The grass is conserving its energy, browning out.
The trees are casting off their spare parts
in disorganized piles.
The no longer flourishing flowers
are being tidied away by the park keepers.
The crackable fountains are empty and dry.

The old woman is also dismantling herself.
Her pinkness is fading.
She is casting off hair and extra skin.
She grows dry and crackly like a potato chip,
preserves herself like a salt fish.
As the storage space inside her
shrinks smaller and tighter
she is casting out names.

Still, you mustn't worry.
She is saving enough space to keep you in:
your color and sound, your essential shape,
the way it feels when a sandwich goes
from your hand into hers, your warm kitchen,
how good it felt to have you in her womb.

She is cleaning out names to make room
for all this. So that even if your name
should be spilled out with the others,
you will be packed away intact.

Another crow flies by. It's hard to keep afloat in this wind and this crow's feathers are in wild disarray. He gives me a baleful glance as he is flung close by my window; a great, disreputable, ominous bird.

UNSEEN SOUND

The fog echoes with unseen noises.
Fragments of sound tumble, foreboding,
among lost molecules of damp.
The call of a voice from a far boat
hollows out a wet halloo.
An invisible splash sounds like an accident,
sends the adrenalin racing,
while fog shrouds the ruptured lake.

On land in the clear dark, voices
have a dry particularity, out of place
like a flock of goats in the city.
Each voice speaks from the dark street
with a clean click. Until at two,
into the clarity a cut voice screams "NO!"
In twos and threes the torturers disband
while over its head the city pulls the dark.
My heart is pounding, knowing that this time
the invisible accident has happened for sure.

DECEMBER

The mild and drowsy waves come in without the energy to break their monotonous formation. Farther out in the lake a few renegade whitecaps protest the regularity: "Hey!" they say, "Jiggle! Get out of line! Wake up!"

6 A.M.

She is waking in the deep weeds of dreams
stalking them sleepily,
a lazy fisher.

She leafs through the dawn sky.
Sometimes she is sucked into rocking waters.
Horizons beckon her.

Sky comes down over her like a silk sheet.
A lake licks her feet.
Sand drifts up to her knees.

She is touched by wind,
lapped in circling currents,
packed in spume.

She is mist gathering into fog,
crystal ice accumulating,
a storm forming.

She is a mirage taking on substance,
a cloud, a wave, a gust of air
nuzzling the morning.

The water is turning sluggish with cold. But the waves come insistently onto the frozen sand; along the edge of the beach they are gradually building a barricade of ice.

CONTEST OF QUIETISM

Her stillness tops his.
He, stiller still,
smothers her quiet
with his own and she
lashes back with silence
so thick it thunders.
He retaliates with peace,
defying her still brain,
until, like wilted balloons,
they both implode with a soft
whoosh and disappear.

The lake keeps me company. It talks to me. It runs cool over my eyes. It tells stories. It shouts when it has to and slams its fist on the beach. Sometimes it giggles with its little lapping edges. Today its teasing mist is back, mysterious, and overexcited.

GHOSTS

The old ghosts left, talking in ordinary voices.
You could hear their heels click on the attic stairs.
They all moved out when I did.
Grandma's ghost took the mildewed carpetbag,
my miser aunt the unused linen towels.
Father took the painting of a swaybacked horse
and Mother, a barely started sketchbook
(two castles and a cow). What a clatter!
They always made their presence felt
with auras and footsteps. It was comforting
to hear them dropping things among the boxes.

This new place has no homey attic
full of aromatic dust and trunks,
and yet, to my surprise, I hear
whispers in my ear, and in my head
there's a familiar rustle in the clutter.

Black branches make thick black lines across the mist. A crow sitting on one of the branches peers into the thin fog. I wonder if he can see farther into it with his differently made bird-eyes than I can see with mine?

SEEING BIRDS

Crazy. Crazy. Slowly it became clear.
Not just uncooperative, or dreamy, or curably
lazy. No help available for crazy.
A brother, slipped out of my grasp.
He talked so hifalutin. How was I, who
had avoided all science, to know
if what he said was brilliant or mad.

But I knew it was wonderful.
He quoted great men whose intricate
minds meandered through his head.
Bertrand Russell would have been
proud to have said the things
my brother said he said.

And he saw visions of raptors.
Once walking in the hospital grounds
in spring, he stopped and looking up
asked me quietly: "See the owl?"
Embarrassed by his hallucinations
I almost didn't look to see
the great bird sleepily scowl down
in disapproval of my disbelief.

With the credibly false and the unbelievably true
hiding among the foliage in his head,
my brother rustled as he walked
through leaves of words.

There are pigeons in gull territory today. A thin skin of ice is moving in the hands of a wind cartographer. He draws maps and constantly corrects them.

THE WINE DARK SEA

I've leaned over the rail
and looked into the Mediterranean Sea
trying to make it wine dark. I want to believe Homer.
But it's always blue or green or gray for me
except at sunset when it might be gold or persimmon.

Now, trying to see the lake's color through your eyes,
I understand that Homer too, was not exactly blind
but had an eye disease which cut out blues and greens
so that the Mediterranean, his sea (and it can be dark),
was dark all rubily, colored truly with blood,
Greeks and Trojans bleeding into his retina.

I will buy rose-colored glasses to warm the cool blues,
to see a lake bloodshot with burgundy and blood
spreading in wine-dark pools over the ice.

The steadily falling snow erases the city grime. It only takes an inch of windless snowfall to leave a clean slate.

DECEMBER 31, 1991

The landscape is a mummy
embossed with silver trees.
It lies embalmed in cold
at the end of a terrible year.

When we spoke up nobody answered.
The trees just squeaked their branches
the way they do on a cold day,
and the silence held its breath.

We stumbled through the year
among burning oil wells
and starving children,
tripping over people asleep in the street.

Tonight is New Year's Eve.
Will the gods join us while we toast tomorrow
in excellent champagne?
Will they throw confetti and sing Auld Lang Syne?

I'm watching the night sky for a GO sign
since we have to cross the rickety bridge
between last year's public disasters
and next year's mandatory hope.

January

Between me and the lake the rush hour traffic thunders by like herds of buffalo. In the evening it stampedes back the other way. But in the small hours of the morning cars are isolated animals prowling beneath the streetlight moons. They go in lonely ones and twos while all night long most cars are tethered in the dark asleep.

BUS TO THE ALBUQUERQUE AIRPORT

A grandmother leans her head against the window,
an old woman sitting on her hands in a dry bus
short of breath and short of temper,
a dry bone rattling.

The tourists remember meals, adjust their clothes,
and set their watches on to real-life time,
as we leave the Sangré range
and Santa Fe behind.

They pass six hot cows lying in the shade
of a solitary tree. The Sandia mountains
lurch past the bus windows,
past the desert glass.

The huge sky casually covers outer space
with a blue substance made of air, a blue
which filters down to fill the lungs
of butterflies and mice.

The beautiful blade of a thin daughter's face,
a child picking and piling strawberries,
a girl trying purple lipstick on
for courage and hope.

She files these mental pictures in her head
with landscapes sandwiched in between.
The jagged Jemez mountains
rumple the horizon.

She's breathed her ration of clear air;
some more of her fair share of God's eternity
is used. She tilts a little
going round a curve.

A woman wrapped in a dark cape sits on a rock at the end of the promontory, watching the city. She sits so still that she seems bewitched. The water beside her breathes under a skin of ice which sudden gusts of wind wrinkle like silk.

MY CHILDHOOD IS MY FIRSTBORN CHILD

The wheels of the bus sang to me
as I rode down Michigan Avenue
feeling like a princess come home
or like a sort of owner.
"This is *my* city," I kept saying.

The old skyscrapers leaned over me
like trees saying hello.
My old aunts smiled and kissed me
and for a while I walked
through the underpass into my childhood
whenever I felt like it.

I went on a spree of remembering
until the ghosts grew tired of prompting me,
and I had to squint to see myself in the zoo.
The child I recorded so tenderly
grew threadbare like an old carpet.

Yet, now and then,
when I'm walking along in my city
thinking of nothing, just smelling winter,
I jump out at myself, knee socks falling,
out from a familiar configuration of buildings,
throwing fistfuls of unnameable feelings
like snow. They settle on my bent shoulders
making my old woman weep with love.

The cold rain is filling all the puddles and the gutters. The streets are running with near-ice and the weatherman is forecasting a freeze. Everyone is fastening cleats to the soles of their boots and all the old ladies are worrying about their bones.

IMAGINING WATER

My daughter lives among the dry
gray green chamiso bushes
on the banks of a river of sand.
Every day she walks up it
towards mountains, and every day
she walks back down to her children
waiting on the banks of the dry arroyo.

I tell my friend and she says:
What about flash floods?
So I begin imagining water rushing,
flinging stones, throwing my daughter
over its torrential shoulders
while her children cry on the banks.

I telephone my daughter in New Mexico
to warn her before it's too late.
She laughs, the way people in deserts
laugh at the idea of water. "And anyway"
she says, "my arroyo doesn't run
in a canyon. I'd just step out of the way."

Something is floating in patches at the edge of the water. Is it seaweed? Dead fish? Garbage? The water looks unshaven, scrofulous under a scum of ice. Patches of rough skin have been mapped into the distance. The gulls look like paper litter blowing in a dirty sky. But the three little diving ducks are as black and white as ever. They dive and disappear and come up clean over and over.

ACHILLES HEEL

When mothers dip their children for their own good,
they have to hold on somewhere
the way Achilles' mother held on to him
when she dipped him in the River Styx.

Though she aims to make him invulnerable all over,
that handhold makes a place to be wounded.
All sorts of things can crawl in through his heel,
like love, or pride, or death from a shifty arrow.

The bronze boy taking a thorn out of his foot
may be blaming his mother.
But I'm thinking that leaving a way in
may have been her best gift.

Cloud shadows mixed with reflections of clouds skid across glare ice. The lake is a sheer frozen pool where gulls land and stand like storks on long reflection-doubled legs.

IN THE OPEN

My mind is fascinated by emptiness:
a floor swept clean
a bathtub without water
a hollow tree
a sheet of paper.
In such a place
one crumb
is an occupation
one ant a family.
My mind works on a wide plain
more easily than in a box of detail.
It glides
fluently roller-blading
to a conclusion.

Looking at the icy lake I have an airplane view of a rough plain with a great river meandering through it. A remote village sits on the far bank where the ice has broken into blocks. Mountains have risen in the distance and fjords jut out from the shore. Today I have an arctic landscape to explore.

THE VISTA MAKERS

Aunts stood by the porch all afternoon
cooperating on the landscape:
here a bush, there a snip with the clippers,
squinting at vistas as they worked.

They arranged trees to delete power lines
from the sunset; the wind blew
in the rigging of the cottonwoods and waves
of grass broke on the banks of the prairie.

    In the evening they watched the changing light
    the way some people listen to music.

Here in the city they have learned to turn
potted geraniums on their city sill
so leaves block out the street light's glare,
and flaming flowers disguise the cold.

Traffic on the street below
foams in their ears like surf, and in the park
Illuminated restrooms built with arches
are little coliseums in the night.

    Each aunt, pretending doggedly, reclines
    into her pruned world like an odalisque.

Huddled blackbirds scattered through the winter tree look like wizened currants. The weather shrivels me too. I don't plump up in this cold pudding.

SHRINKING AND STRETCHING

All the spaces inside which used to be big enough
are shrinking to puddles like reservoirs in a drought.
There is rationing and the faucets just drip.

I do stretching exercises
trying to open the sluice gates wider
so pools will expand into lakes.

I try to breathe each cell open, to expand
its capacity. I lengthen myself,
begging my tendons, imploring my muscles

so that, when the cloudburst comes
there'll be space to store the water
and it won't spill off into storm gutters
as muddy tears, too salty for watering.

I'm thinking of travelers on this steaming lake: Marquette and Joliet watching the lake make clouds to shroud canoes in secrecy, La Salle and Tonte on their serious camping trip paddling past the ancestors of these ducks. The lake had already been a road for voyagers, taking them to places which recorded their bodies and their bones and carefully preserved their manufactured stones.

I imagine these men out there canoeing fast through a camouflage of mist.

LOST NAME

A steep climb
over sharp stones.
Mother forgot the sandwiches
and our bottle of water
but we huffed on
no breath to complain.
  *(I am turning out my memory
  for the name of the mountain.)*

When we stopped to rest
the Baedeker in Father's pocket
comforted us with stories.
  "...the Springs of Forgetting and Remembering
  bubble out of clefts in this mountain."
My father turned the thin old pages
and asked my mother which she'd pick?
She took off her shoes and zap!
with her feet in a bunch of grass,
she chose the Spring of Forgetting.
  *(I am wringing my memory
  for the name of the mountain.)*

In those days I remembered what I knew.
Names of mountains ran out of my mouth
like big and little children. Words
came easy and life was for collecting
things to remember. I had not yet done anything
worth bothering to forget...And there
sat my mother on a Greek rock,
choosing to forget instead of remember!
What terrible things had she seen and done?

Now I am her wary age, steering
between things I have learned to forget,
searching for things I need to remember.

I lie in wait for the name of the mountain
like a cat in ambush. I creep stealthily
over the jagged stones and...pounce!

Parnassus! Parnassus! Parnassus!

FEBRUARY

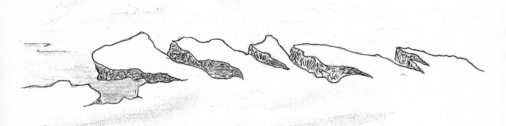

The bay is full of sparkling ice. There are ice dunes at the edge of the expanded beach. Its rough spackle of frozen sand is pocked with snow. Black branches are printed on white. The bay looks dead though it shines back like crushed glass. Where will the cold stop? What will it finally include?

There is nothing to show that the world still goes until one reassuring gull, flying very high and far away, comes alone into the frozen world, and then, along the sidewalk, one walker, collar pulled up to his ears, hat down over his eyebrows, hands deep in his pockets, hunches himself against the cold.

THE SPARTAN MOTHER

Where she came from, close calls were even less to cry about
than spilt milk. After a close shave a good child laughed it off.
Everything was patched with maxims. Platitudes were
    bandaids.
A cry-baby reaped his just reward. Don't look back, and never
cross your bridges until you come to them.

When the girl fell off the slippery roof
she had a narrow squeak of course, but nothing broke. Why
    cry?
When the scythe hanging on the wall fell so near the young
    man's eye
it was only a close shave. No need to make a fuss.
When the car skidded out of control into a gentle snowbank
"Why do you scream?" they asked, annoyed.

So she grew up, calloused about hair's-breadth escapes.
It's only lately, when her daughter telephones too late or too
    early,
That she wonders if misses really are as good as miles?

There is ice all over. Snow fills the frozen bumps with white. The lake closes out the world with a shut face. So, in my mind, I go out through the snow with a long pole and bang on the ice. "Open up!" I say, trying for even a small hole so I can lean over it and listen to water splash. But nothing moves. The ice is too thick for my stick to crack.

THE DEAF MAN"S WIFE

She shouts "I am here!"
He smiles softly and
after a pause, speaks:
"I will," he says.

The mute cat
deepens the silence,
a secret drinker,
it drinks only found water.

She proves the philosopher right:
"laughing makes you happy,
crying makes you sad,
loud speaking hardens you."

Twitching against the light
the cat's ears listen
as the wife lays siege
to the deaf man's enclosure.

Soft talk
can turn her gentle.
She needs the cat
to speak to quietly.

Today the surprised gulls stand on sculptures of ripples. An ampersand of current still connects the frozen bay with movement, and still farther out archipelagoes of ice sway heavily. But in the bay where there is not the smallest breath of wind on water, I can see all of yesterday's motion memorized in ice.

THE MODEL

The statue my mother makes in her studio
is me. The real me is in tears
being read to by my grandmother,
being fed peppermints while I pose.
But the statue is nicer than me.
She makes it so lovingly.
She cares about how I look, too,
but I never look right,
and she can't change me
by tipping her head to one side,
squinting, and then sticking on
another little piece of clay.

The bird framed by my window flies south. For a couple of seconds the window contains its flight completely, and makes a picture of a bird in flight. The bird reaches the frame and disappears behind it. I watch for it to reappear in the window just to the right but it doesn't show up. It's flown itself disturbingly invisible.

UNDER THE BED

My babysitting grandmother called:
"Yoo Hoo! Time to get up now."
On some kind of impulse to be bad,
I got under the bed instead.
When she saw my empty room,
no napping child, my thin grandmother
with her hair flying out of its net
rushed to the edge of the ocean outside.

I could hear her crying and calling,
expecting my drowned body to wash up.
When it didn't, she began climbing the rockfall
behind our summer cottage
looking for a fallen mangled child.
Calling. Weeping. Louder all the time.

Terrified by the sound of my grandmother's
grief for lost me, I stayed put
in the sandy dust, bad past hope
until the down-to-earth cook knelt
and aimed the comforting shine of her eyes
into my dusty dark.

What a relief it was to be found,
not dead after all!

Once, while I was young, I lived on a still pond that was sometimes too motionless to bear. The lake I watch while I'm old always shows at least some sign of life: a ripple here and there, snow flurries, steam rising. It's the sky I can't bear now, when it looks at me out of one huge blind eye, saying nothing.

RETIRED

The light dies among old men
patiently sitting in a ghostly afterlife
on chintz settees, and Good Night comes
on rubber soles to old women waiting politely
on nice furniture in the death camp of age,
disempowered, bowdlerized, patiently smiling their
way into dementia, that terrible anaesthetic.

I talk to myself like Thomas to his father:
Do not go gentle! Please keep the dignity of rage.

Sometimes I think that only the angry
lead their lives to the end, pacing like lions
up and down the furnished halls. Awake
until it's dark, they push their way
past those who gentle them. Still tossing
the hot potato 'I' from hand to hand,
and juggling it with love, they burn and burn.

I talk to myself like Thomas to his father:
Do not go gentle! Please keep the dignity of rage.

The waves gather out of the shadow a cloud has spread on the water. They rise, lift to a sharp rim, and seem to move towards the beach. But, for some reason, however high they grow, they can't break. I've read that when a wave moves forward it's only the motion that moves; each molecule of water stays pretty much in the same place.

So I watch the optical illusion of moving water, waiting for the moment when the water crests and cracks and some of the broken wave breaks free in a foaming rush.

ON THE DOCK
For a Sailor Dying of Cancer

Your children remind me of the trees
brought in pots from China to make lumber
for the trim on clipper ships, or to make shadows
over the captain's wife on her doorstep.

Now they are watching you and the ocean.
All of your daughters and each of your sons
sit with you on the dock, all dangling their legs
in the same familiar water.
The dinghy thumps gently at the pilings.

Mostly it happens in silence:
the spread of pain to a new place
the new medicine to cool it working
or not working, a fresh chance.
At first dying is a shuttle ferry
not a firm departure. He moves towards it
in spurts and snatches, always
coming back with a cheerful toot on his horn
but frailer, like a boat damaged by ice,
a boat not built for ice, as no body is.

The ropes we hold are getting frayed,
nobody can help noticing though we don't mention it.
Pulling on them doesn't do any good
so we just hang on with slipping hands
and talk quietly and look out to sea
while you hope and stay and leave
all at the same time.

I didn't see the crow fall into the water. When I looked out my window his feathers were already soggy and his unwebbed feet were clawing at the lake. For a while the desperate flopping of his wings against the suction of the water kept him upright and afloat. His wings acted as outriggers as long as he could beat them.

But he wasn't alone. Another crow circled over him, giving an occasional close swoop of encouragement. She couldn't fish him out of the water, but she stayed as near him as she could, until after a while the drowning bird looked up at her and sank, beak last.

THE VISIT

I travel to see my husband
who hasn't been my husband for a long time.
I climb his porch steps
hoping his wife won't be at the new door.

Blind and gently swinging
silently waiting (he knew I was coming)
the porch swing rocks
as he pushes his runner's toes against the floor.

I see him waiting behind opaque eyes
in his blind dark. Although he was always thin,
cancer, like a tanner,
has stretched him taut over his bones.

When he hears the creak of the steps
he turns the echo of his old face to me
and smiles like a radiant dry leaf.
He finds my hand and guides me

into the dark house for fragrant tea,
opens the door deftly. The invisible wife
has left the teapot and the cups and saucers out.
He pours my tea. Pulls up a shade

so light reflects from both our faces.
We sit on old familiar chairs,
talking about pain. Or is it love?
The pattern on the teacups says *Hello!*

MARCH

At sunrise there's a small break in the humdrum sky.
Four gulls are flying towards this pink place. Maybe they can
get through and find the sun which hasn't been out for days.

AUTOBIOGRAPHY

She sits in bed before breakfast
chasing escaping dreams among the bedclothes.
She is composing her life as well as she can,
finding discarded pieces and fitting them in.
She sorts and labels. She revises some of her relatives.
Ones she had thought were the main characters
turn incidental as she slides slippery fugitives
into stories she had remembered differently.

Every night she casts sleep like a net.
Hauled in when she wakes,
it may hold one fat first grader
or an uncle eating an egg.
She may pull up a dripping merchild of memory
who sits on a tall stool under a skylight
shaking the water off her tail.

Every day she is working the story nearer
to truth. Sometimes a dark corner
needs to be lit up or a soft footstep put in.
She sits in her bed looking for reasons:
why the house in the dream seemed to be underwater—
why her brother lay on the ground and didn't hit back—
which of the people coming down the stairs
were really there at all— She is handling shadows.

She sits in bed in the morning, hindsight honed by sleep,
trying to make a true-to-life self
out of a person who won't stand still.
She's sortingseventy years into a story
whose plot will make sense
when the last line finally takes place.

The cauldron is steaming into the cold.
Full of snails and fish, peppered with ducks,
salted with floating gulls, today
the bay is a bowl of bouillabaisse.

ON BEING TOLD THAT I HAVE TO USE A CANE

My inner eye cuts to a vision of my father
prancing to his cane's swing
through the Sunday park
on a frosty day of near-spring.
My mitten freezes
to my father's glove.
The air crackles and he says,
"Hup! Hup! Hup!
Breathe deep and suck up your gut!"
and we march
to the click
of his metronome stick.
Or he swings it up
and it pauses there
at the peak of the air
with a hesitation—
a syncopation. I skip
to the beat of its pause.
It can reach up
to part twigs in a tree
so we can see
the bird he's heard
through the hole
his cane has made
or it can probe into warm March wet
and feel by the depth it goes
whether it's spring yet.
When it's time for lunch
he stands in the street,
his cane a command.
The obedient cars wait
while I cross on proud feet.

Oh, to have such a strong stick!

There's a flotilla of ice clouds floating on the lake. They look like Georgia O'Keefe's picture of clouds: little snowy floaters, decreasing in size with distance. They have holes in their middles eaten out by the water. Doughnuts maybe, or sweet ice.

TWELVE-YEAR-OLD GIRLS READING
KEATS' ST. AGNES EVE IN 1934

In our school dictionary we looked up the "gules"
thrown by the moon on Madeline's fair breast
and memorized Porphyro's sensuous wait
in the secret closet of her room.
I, fat and always hungry, learned more of love
from lucent syrups tinct with cinnamon,
jellies soother than the creamy curd
and candied apples, than from the rich attire
creeping to her knees. My friend,
with small points on her chest, got more
out of his warm unnerved arm
sunk in the blanched linen of her bed
and, seriously more musical than I,
out of the tender chords and hollow lute.
But when, like a throbbing star, into her dream
he melted and the rose blended its odor
with the violet (solution sweet),
we weren't quite sure...Could Keats
be saying what he seemed to say
right there in public in the book
our English teacher had told us to read?

Today the water ends at the horizon with such clarity that it seems to be inviting the sky to dive in, and the sky is so clear that it looks like an invitation to the lake to take off and fly. You can look straight into the future with the farseeing eyes of a falcon.

FEEDING ON LANDSCAPE

She sits at the window, greedily seeing,
gulping down light and shadow.
Into her hungry eyes she stuffs the downswing of birdflight
as birds fold themselves into the morning.
The air outside is a feast of gulls flying.

The man with empty eyes stands at the window
while she tries to feed him the gymnastic
breakers, telling how they leap in this strong wind
to lick the icing off the cakes of cut rock.

But when he opens the window wide
he can hear the water boiling,
and taste the smell of waves.
With its rough hands,
the wind serves him a rich soup.

Near shore the patchwork of snow, dark water, and gray velvet ice make a palomino lake. Beyond the breakwater the gray turns lavender and spreads in wide soft stripes between strips of pale blue watered silk. All the shades of white are lying there asleep.

SLEEP

Sleep is a skill tired people have
sitting in a traffic jam,
or the waiting room of a delayed doctor,
or in a stalled train.

The other passengers may laugh at you,
but it's cheap and handy,
full of whiteness and softness,
ready to take you in.
If you're good at it
you can curl up in it quietly,
or, still sitting,
you can wrap it around you.

If the airplane you are traveling on
sits on the runway for hours,
you needn't listen to the intercom
clearing its throat and trying
to comfort you with promises.
Just close your eyes and find
the runway to your own airport.
Let yourself out. Take off.

If I decided to walk out on the frozen plain which stares at me, if I put cleats on my boots and put on all the coats I have in order to keep warm, even if I walked as delicately as I could, it wouldn't work. I don't know how to walk on such thin ice. I'd drown.

LULLABY FOR A SCHIZOPHRENIC

Sleep in the wind, little brother,
in the buffeting air.
Though it belly you out like sail
and rampage in your hair,
lie curled in your shell,
hand cupped under your ear.
Take off fear like a shirt.

The whirlwind won't wake you,
the tempest won't shake you,
little brother,

asleep in the wind.

APRIL

The lake is suddenly fishing out its colors and filling up with blues and greens. Where could they come from? The leaden sky isn't helping and the trees haven't any green to contribute yet. Maybe the color was stored underwater waiting for spring. Something has suddenly triggered these spasms of aquamarine.

THE MONET SHOW

"...and that is a sort of hill," he says,
"and right behind on the right hand side
there's part of another and in between—
I think it's a river running through.
The top is blue or maybe pink
if I shut this eye. But what's that thing
on top of the hill—that roundish blob?
A tree, you say? Well it looks to me
like more of a house. Yes, I think it's a house.
If I lean up close with my reading glasses
it's easy to see the strokes of paint."
He reaches for the texture of the scene
but stops. The guard shifts feet uneasily,
and people passing pause in wonder
hearing an old man, leaning towards the pictures,
describing the obvious aloud.

Willing himself to see he sees.
His left eye fills in pinks, his right the green
and if he shuts the left the lines are straight
the tree trunks true though faint,
the blank spots on the canvas few.
"Monet—The Series Paintings," or his hand
held up to block the left eye, he will stop
a long time, teasing paintings out of paint,
a man refusing to be blind, assembling Monets.

And she remembers how, in the morning,
as soon as it is light enough to see,
he leans above her, putting her together:
a nose, two eyes, a mouth—he feels to check—
and when he's finally composed her face,
painted the woman that he thinks she is,
he smiles at tears he doesn't see.

If a painter were setting out to paint the lake today, he'd need molten steel, iron filings, oxidized copper and a dash of silver and gold. A clever artist could steal the steel from the mills, the iron from the ore boats, and copper from the flashings on old roofs, and surely someone would give him a silver pitcher and a gold ring in order to see how the picture would turn out.

GARY

Lit by sunrise
the long ore boat
cuts along the line
drawn with a ruler
between water and sky.

Far across the water
smokes a small silhouette
outlined in gold. Its mills
are gilded, the smoke
from its little black chimneys

rises in rosy plumes.
Dirty city! You should
see yourself now,
all gussied up with dawn
for your sweet ore.

There are hunters and gatherers in this city. Men stand in the doors of their fishing shacks out on the harbor ice warming their hands over cans of fire. In late spring old women gather dandelion greens in the park, people shine lights on the water and fish for alewives in the dark, and from April to November people sit in the sun on breakwaters and promontories dangling their lines in the water and waiting for bites.

ARMCHAIR VELDT

You think the giraffe is a graceless animal?
Have you seen her breathtaking
slow-motion lope across Africa,
the long gawkiness turned into flexible floating?
She has such lank appendages to wave
like banners blowing between thorn trees.

Sitting in a darkened room
watching a screenful of giraffes,
my muscles and joints become fluid.
By osmosis, through the membrane
of the TV screen, I soar from awkwardness
to grace, and billow giraffe-like
over the carpet of my living room.

This morning the near shore is the only border of a great horizonless space. If it weren't for the reflection of a single tree there would be no way to tell that the sky doesn't reach down all the way to the rocks. So I play a game with the view. I imagine that the horizon is really higher than it is. This makes the lake into a great upsloping plane and I slither up it like a princess on a glass mountain. At the top a cracked cloud leaves a rosy gap which I wriggle through out of the blankness, into the story. Three birds flutter past the window for punctuation.

TRANSFORMATIONS

The book of Zen pictures lies open on a stool
in the bathroom. When I sit there
in the near dark, only the street light lit,
I see a great dollop of liquid light on the page.
Later, at dawn, it looks like a pear.
But when I look in the morning, the picture
has turned into a monk playing with cymbals,
drawn on a pippala leaf.
In daylight I see every vein in the leaf
although I've never heard of a pippala tree.

The fog is thick. I decide to lie down on it. I cup my hands and swim, trusting it to hold my weight. I soak it up like oil. No ducks. No gulls. No sun. No wind. I am alone in nothing. After a while, still swimming, I begin to dissolve. But luckily my clothes catch on a tree and the rough touch of the branches reconstitutes me. I slither down the trunk, scratched and scraped back into myself, and walk briskly home over the snow.

THE DREAM FISHER

She is loitering at the edge of sleep.
Dawn breezes rearrange her. She senses
great winds in the distance. Her body is filled
with air, buoyant among phantoms.
She is mist brushed by feathers,
soared through by untouchable gulls.

Pieces of dreams scud across her like skimmers.
Anemones rise from the floor of her mind,
flap their ruffles, and soar unidentified into the dark.
Handfuls of minnows slide past her
leaving unreadable silver words on her sides.

She floats up a dune and settles in the dip
beyond its crest. She remembers that someone
thinks she is water. She catches a whiff of desert
as it dissolves riderless
into currents of heat swirling up her brain.

She's looking for the child she saw
holding out a parachute full of holes,
the grass telling about too little rain,
the camel, who laid his nose against her knee
and said, "Even I, sometimes, need water."

But as the night leaks out of its rusty bucket
she only catches thimblefuls
of what it told her. All she remembers
in the morning, is the sense of a two-toed hoof
making a print in sand.

The wind has changed. The trees are bending in a different direction. Birds are flying north, and I am swept with the feeling that I can steer to somewhere that is not an accident.

SPOTLIGHT

It is a small storm.
Birds tumble in the wind.
When a few clouds break open over the lake

a spotlight blazes on an invisible performer.
I peer into the dazzle of someone
shimmering on an unsteady stage.

Père Marquette paddling down from Canada?
A swimmer testing his strength?
Somebody walking on water?

The shutter stays open in the sky,
and for a moment the important unseen
dances on the whitecaps.

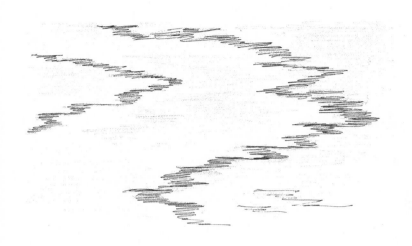

Alice Ryerson Hayes lives with her husband Albert Hayes in Chicago, the city where she grew up. She lived for many years in Cambridge, Massachusetts, where she was a school psychologist and a student of archeology. She returned to the Chicago area and founded the Ragdale Foundation, an artists' colony in Lake Forest, in a house designed by her grandfather, noted architect Howard Shaw. She has published three previous books of poetry, and many of her poems have appeared in literary magazines. She has four children and eight grandchildren.